FESTIVE OCCASIONS

Judy Ridgway

Oxford University Press

Contents

Oxford University Press, Walton Street, Oxford OX2 6DP

Oxford   New York   Toronto
Delhi   Bombay   Calcutta   Madras   Karachi
Petaling Jaya   Singapore   Hong Kong   Tokyo
Nairobi   Dar es Salaam   Cape Town
Melbourne   Auckland

and associated companies in
Berlin   Ibadan

Oxford is a trade mark of Oxford University Press

© Judy Ridgway 1986
First published 1986
Reprinted 1987, 1988
ISBN 0 19 832730 7

Typeset by Tradespools Ltd., Frome, Somerset
Printed in Hong Kong

Introduction

All over the world people celebrate the special days and festivals of their different cultures and religions. They also remember important dates in their past history.

Very often these celebrations take the form of people gathering together in families and in their places of worship and prayer. Sometimes the occasion demands serious thought and doing without food, but more often the celebrations are joyful.

After the religious ceremonies are over, people often join each other for a special meal. To mark the occasion the very best food which people can afford is served.

This book looks at thirty festivals. Some of them have a religious background. Others are based on historical events. Where there are traditional foods which are easy to make, these have been included in the recipe sections. In other cases there are no special dishes, and recipes are given which are typical of the country or peoples concerned.

New Year

New Year celebrations in Trafalgar Square

The end of the old year and the beginning of the new year is a time for celebration everywhere.

January is named after Janus, the Roman God, who was in charge of beginnings, doors, and entrances. He was able to look backwards and forwards at the same time. The Romans liked to think of him doing that at the close of the old year and the start of the new one.

All over the Western World people still do just this. Parties are held which go on past midnight on New Year's Eve. Toasts can then be drunk to the New Year as soon as the clock shows that 1st January has begun.

In Scotland these celebrations are called Hogmanay, and in some parts Cake Day. Indeed, a rich biscuit-type cake is traditionally served at New Year. It is shortbread and it is made with butter, sugar, and white flour.

Many of the Scottish traditions of Hogmanay have been taken up by people in other parts of the British Isles. In London crowds gather in Trafalgar Square. Everyone starts to cross arms, link hands, and sing *Auld Lang Syne.* This song was written by Robert Burns about two hundred years ago.

In the North of England and in Scotland the custom of "first footing" is felt to be very important. The first person to enter the house after midnight on New Year's Eve is known as the "first-footer". To ensure good luck for the household the first-footer should be male, young, healthy, and good looking. He ought to be dark haired, and he should be carrying a small piece of coal or charcoal, money, bread, and salt. These are all symbols of prosperity. Unfortunately, folklore insists that blond or red-headed men are out, and that women first-footers are unlucky!

The traditions of January are connected with the old winter festivities enjoyed by the Norsemen in Scandinavia long ago. These usually involved time or light, and were thought to encourage the sun to return. In some parts of Scotland and Northumberland there are still parades in the streets with lighted torches. In Holland many people burn Christmas trees on street bonfires and let off fireworks.

Petticoat Tails

This is a thinner, crisper version of the traditional Scottish shortbread. It was popular with the ladies of both the Scottish and French courts in the fifteenth century. Its name probably comes from the French name "petites galettes".

Ingredients
100 g butter
75 g icing sugar
175 g plain flour

Equipment
mixing bowl
wooden spoon
rolling pin
baking tray

Method

1 Set the oven to 170°C/325°F/Gas 3.
2 Cream the butter with a wooden spoon. Gradually beat in the icing sugar, adding 25 g at a time.
3 Add the flour in one go. Knead into the mixture with your hands to form a smooth dough.
4 Grease a baking tray and place the dough on this.
  Roll out to form a circle.
  Then press out with your fingers to make a thin round 25 cm in diameter.
  Cut round a large dinner plate if you want a smooth finish.
5 Mark the top into 8 portions by scoring lightly with a knife.
6 Mark the edges into notches with the handle of a dinner knife.
7 Prick the top all over with a fork.
8 Bake for 20–25 minutes until golden in colour.
9 Leave to cool on the tin.
  Cut into fans to serve.

Makes 8 triangles.

Variation

For the more traditional kind of shortbread, use castor sugar instead of icing sugar. Continue the recipe as for Petticoat Tails, but do not press the dough out quite so thinly. Bake at 180°C/350°F/Gas 4 until golden.

Chinese New Year

Chinese dragon in Hong Kong procession

The old Chinese calendar was different from the Western calendar. It was based on the movements of the moon. Each time a new moon appeared, a new month began. This made the Chinese year ten days shorter than the Western year, which is based on the movements of the sun. The moon-based year is called a "lunar" year and the sun-based year a "solar" year. The difference between the two kinds of years was made up by adding an extra month to the lunar year every two or three years.

Each Chinese year carries the name of an animal. According to legend, twelve animals answered a call from Buddha. These were the rat, ox, tiger, rabbit, dragon, snake, horse, ram, monkey, cockerel, dog, and pig. The years are named after each animal in turn. People born in each year are thought to be like the animal for which it is named.

The date of the Chinese New Year changes every year, but it always falls between 21st January and 20th February. Preparations for the festivities begin well in advance. Ten days before the event householders and shopkeepers start by cleaning out their premises, and special fairs are held each evening to sell flowers or paintings, drawings, and crockery decorated with flowers.

On New Year's Eve, all the family gather together at home to see in the New Year. Outside, the celebrations begin on the stroke of midnight. Firecrackers explode in the street to frighten away the spirits of the old year.

In the Chinese areas of London, and in other large cities of Britain, the local Chinese people celebrate the New Year with processions through the streets. These are led by friendly dragons which knock on each door. The owner of each house or business opens the door to welcome in good luck, rather like the "first-footer" is welcomed in Scotland.

Special festive treats are served at this time. They include bowls of peanuts, melon seeds, and preserved fruits. Each of these has a special significance such as good fortune, long life, and happiness. These ingredients are also used to make special biscuits and stuffed cakes.

New Year Cookies

These New Year Cookies use the traditional New Year foods. They are a symbol of good luck. They are sold all over China, in the Chinese quarter of London, and in other cities in the West.

Here is a recipe for making them at home.

Ingredients

25 g raw peanuts
1 tablespoon sesame
   seeds
100 g butter or
   margarine

100 g sugar
1 egg
175 g rice flour
50 g cornflour
25 g dates (optional)

Equipment

baking tray
bakewell or
   greaseproof paper
grill pan

kitchen knife
tablespoon
fork, wooden spoon
mixing bowl

Method

1 Set the oven to 180°C/350°F/Gas 4 and line a baking tray with bakewell or greaseproof paper.
2 Toast the peanuts under the grill until golden in colour, and chop finely.
3 Next toast the sesame seeds until golden, and mix with the nuts.
4 Cream the butter or margarine with the sugar until light and fluffy.
   Beat in the egg, adding a little flour if the mixture shows signs of curdling.
5 Add the flours and the nut and sesame mixture and mix to a dough.
   You will have to use your hands for the last stages of the mixing.
6 Wash, dry, and flour your hands, and divide the mixture into 12–14 balls.
   Shape into cookies about 6–7 cm in diameter and ½ cm thick.
   If using dates press into the centre of each ball and fold over the dough.
   Shape into a cookie with no date showing.
7 Place on the baking tray.
   Bake for 12–15 minutes.

Makes 12–14.

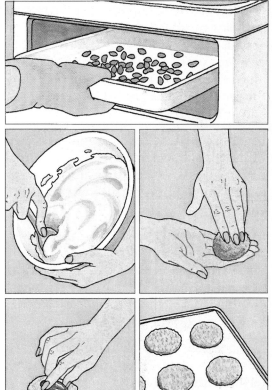

Meelad-al-Nabil

The Ka'bah in Mecca

This is the celebration of the birth of the Prophet Muhammad. It is a very important day in the Muslim calendar. The actual date of the festival varies from year to year, for the Muslims use a "lunar" calendar based on the phases of the moon. However, it usually falls at the end of February or early in March.

Muslims believe in one God, Allah. Muhammad is their Prophet. His birthday is marked by feasting and rejoicing and by the retelling of the story of his life and beliefs.

Muhammad was born in the Quraysh tribe of Arabs in Mecca, a town on the hot, barren highlands of Arabia, running next to the Red Sea. He had a normal childhood, though his parents died when he was quite young.

He became a trader and married a wealthy widow. This gave him some leisure time to think about the evils of his society and about the religious teachings he had heard both at home, and on his travels.

When he was 40, Muhammad began to wander about the lonely hills near Mecca. One day, as he was praying in a cave at the foot of Mount Hira, he had a vision of the Archangel Gabriel. The angel told him to go out and preach that there was only one God and that he, Muhammad, was His Prophet who was to reform the world.

To start with Muhammad was unsure of himself and full of doubt. But, after months of prayer, he accepted that he had indeed heard the word of God. He knew that it was his duty to pass on the message he had received.

Muhammad could not write. So he memorized the teachings which God had given to him. He spoke them in the streets and market places of his home town. His ideas were not popular. Many traders made their livings by serving the pilgrims who came to worship many gods and goddesses at the Ka'bah in Mecca. Because Muhammad taught that there was only one God, some of the traders thought this would harm their business. So they decided to kill him.

The danger was so great that Muhammad had to hide in a cave and then flee to Medina. This successful escape is called the Hijra and is celebrated at the start of the Islamic year.

However, Muhammad's teachings won more and more followers and he returned to Mecca. The Ka'bah was emptied of its idols and rededicated to the one true God, whom Muslims call Allah.

After Muhammad's death in AD 632, all his prophecies and sayings were collected and written down in the Muslim "bible" or Quran.

Lamb with Okra Casserole

Muslim families in Britain usually eat the food of their native land at the main meal of a festival day. This could mean curry and rice for Asian families or lamb with okra for a Middle Eastern family. Okra is a many-sided seed pod which is eaten as a vegetable. Green beans can be used instead of okra if this is difficult to find.

Muslims never eat pork. The meat which they do eat must be butchered so that all the blood is removed. So in all towns where there is a Muslim community you will find a "Halal" butcher who prepares the meat according to Muslim custom.

Ingredients

450 g okra or green beans	1 tablespoon tomato purée
1 tablespoon cooking oil	1 tablespoon lemon juice
600 g lean lamb, cut into pieces	¼ teaspoon allspice salt and black pepper
2 large tomatoes	

Equipment

frying pan	kitchen knife
small casserole with lid	sieve
	spoons

Method

1 Set the oven to 180°C/350°F/Gas 4.
2 Wash and dry the vegetables.
   Cut the stalks off the okra, taking care not to cut into the pod
   or top and tail the beans and cut into lengths.
3 Fill the base of the casserole with the vegetables.
4 Heat the oil in the frying pan.
   Lightly fry the lamb pieces in the oil until the lamb is brown on all sides.
   Arrange the meat on top of the vegetables.
5 Prepare the tomatoes by plunging them into boiling water for a minute.
   Skin with a knife.

6 Rub the tomatoes through the sieve and mix with the tomato purée, lemon juice, allspice, salt, and pepper.
   Spread over the top of the meat.
7 Cover the casserole and bake for 1 hour, until the meat is tender and the vegetables are soft.
8 Serve with boiled rice.

Serves 4.

Boiled Rice

Ingredients
225 g long grain rice
450 ml water
salt

Equipment
saucepan with lid
fork

Method

1 Place the rice and water in a saucepan together with the salt.
2 Bring to the boil.
   Stir once and cover with a lid.
3 Reduce the heat and cook for 15 minutes until all the liquid has been taken up.
4 Remove from the heat and leave to stand with the lid on for 5 minutes.
5 Fluff up with a fork and serve.

Serves 4.

St Valentine's Day

A Victorian Valentine card

This is the day when young men send Valentine cards to the girls they love or would like to have as girl-friends. These cards are not signed and nowadays are just as often sent by girls to boys.

St. Valentine's Day is on 14th February, but it is doubtful if many people who send cards ever know who St. Valentine was. In fact, he was a Christian priest who was put to death for his faith by the Roman Emperor Claudius II in AD 270.

He was known as the "apostle of true love" because he secretly performed the Christian marriage ceremony for Roman soldiers who were forbidden to marry by Claudius. The story goes that when he was thrown into prison he fell in love with his gaoler's daughter. On the day he was put to death, he left a little note for her signed "Your Valentine".

The church probably chose this time of year to honour St. Valentine in the hope that it would take the place of a pre-Christian, "pagan" festival of which it disapproved. This was the Roman festival of Lupercalia. On this day young men chose a girl by a sort of lottery system, and the girls could not be sure which boy they would get. Today Valentine cards are often left unsigned so that the person who receives it will also be unsure who sent it.

In Elizabethan times Valentines were chosen by drawing lots. The gentleman then had to buy his Valentine an expensive present. This custom died out in the eighteenth century and hand-made cards replaced the presents. These cards were made throughout Victorian times. Nowadays, about a million Valentine cards are bought and sent through the post.

A modern Valentine card

10

Savoury Hearts

Traditionally everything must be heart-shaped for St. Valentine's Day, so here's a fun snack that's appropriate for the day.

Ingredients

2 large slices wholemeal bread
2 long spring onions
50 g grated Cheddar cheese

knob butter
1 tablespoon water
1 teaspoon tomato ketchup
salt and pepper

Equipment

1 small saucepan
wooden spoon
kitchen knife

tablespoon
teaspoon

Method

1 Cut the slices of bread into a heart shape. If you have difficulty with this draw the heart on a piece of paper and cut it out. Place the piece of paper on the bread and cut round it.
2 Toast the slices of bread on each side.
3 Slit the green end of the spring onion to resemble the feather of an arrow.
4 Make a small hole in one side of each piece of toast and push the spring onion "arrow" through, leaving the "arrow head" underneath.
5 Place the cheese and butter in a saucepan.
6 Mix in the water, tomato ketchup, and seasonings.
   Mix to a paste and heat gently.
7 When the mixture is completely smooth, spoon on to the heart-shaped toast and spread right up to the edges.
8 Place the toasts on a grill pan and place under a hot grill.
   Leave until lightly browned and bubbly. Serve at once.

Serves 2.

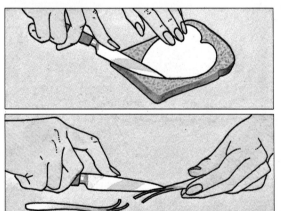

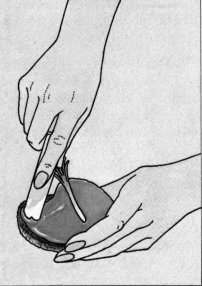

11

Purim

Children getting ready to act out the Purim story

Purim is one of the happiest of the Jewish festivals. As it approaches, in late February or early March, everyone forgets their troubles and starts to make preparations for the holiday. The reason for this is that Purim is a reminder of how the Jewish people living in Persia were saved from destruction.

Years ago, in ancient Persia, a wicked man named Haman wanted to kill all the Jews in the Persian Empire because he thought that one Jew called Mordecai had not shown him proper respect.

Haman was the favourite minister of the king and was very important. So a day was set for the massacre to take place. However, Mordecai had a foster daughter named Esther who was also the second wife of the king. She saved the Jews by making Haman drink too much wine at a banquet. The Jews defeated those who wanted to destroy them and the next day celebrated their victory over Haman and his allies.

Mordecai and Esther were so happy that they vowed that the festival of Purim should be repeated every year for all time. The story of the part which Esther played in the victory is told in the synagogue and at a celebration meal held in every Jewish home on that day.

At the Purim feast special foods are served. These are different in each country but turkey is sometimes chosen for the main course. The turkey is considered to be a stupid animal, and the king of Persia was a foolish king.

Purim is the last festival in the Jewish calendar before Passover. During Passover everyone must clear their houses of flour and bread from the previous year. Purim is a useful time to use up some of that flour. So plenty of cake and biscuits are baked.

At Purim money is given to the poor, and gifts of baked foods and fruit are exchanged. In Eastern Europe the baked foods may be strudels, in the Middle East they may be pastries filled with chopped nuts and oozing with honey, in other countries they may be biscuits made with ground nuts. These biscuits are called Hamantaschen, after the king's favourite minister, or Purim biscuits.

12

Purim Biscuits

In some countries these biscuits are cut into shapes to look like Haman's ears. But most people cut them into triangular or round shapes.

Ingredients

50 g butter, softened
50 g sugar
75 g plain flour
20 g ground almonds or ground hazelnuts
½ teaspoon cinnamon

Equipment

wooden spoon
mixing bowl
baking tray
teaspoon

Method

1 Preheat the oven to 180°C/350°F/Gas 4.
2 Lightly flour an ungreased baking tray.
3 Beat the butter and sugar together in a bowl.
4 Gradually add the flour, a little at a time and knead well together.
5 Knead in the nuts.
6 When the dough feels smooth, roll into small balls the size of walnuts and pat into round biscuit shapes about 3 cm across.
7 Place well apart on the tray.
8 Sprinkle the centre of each biscuit with a little cinnamon.
9 Bake for 15–20 minutes.
   Take care not to let the biscuits get too brown.
   Remove from the oven and cool on a wire rack.

Makes 10–12.

Chick-peas with Tomatoes

Chick-peas are a traditional Purim food. Esther did not eat the rich food served at the Persian court. To be sure of keeping the Jewish food laws, she ate only fruit and vegetables. The chick-peas served at the Purim feast are in remembrance of Esther's respect for the Jewish food laws.

Ingredients

1 × 400 g can chick-peas
4 tomatoes
1 small onion, sliced
1 teaspoon tomato purée
salt and pepper

Equipment

small saucepans
knife
wooden spoon

Method

1 Drop the tomatoes into a pan of boiling water and quickly remove.
   This helps to make the skins easier to peel.
2 Peel and chop the tomatoes.
   Place in a pan with the sliced onion and seasoning.
   Pour in the contents of the can of chick-peas.
3 Bring the mixture to the boil.
   Cover with a lid and simmer for 30 minutes, stirring occasionally.
4 Eat hot or cold.

Serves 2–3.

Carnival

A Carnival float in Brazil

In many Christian countries, the last few days before Lent are the excuse for general merry-making. People dress up in fancy dress or wear masks to disguise themselves, and there may be dancing and singing in the streets.

Carnival was originally an old Italian festival which lasted from Twelfth Night after Christmas to Ash Wednesday.

Today Carnival takes many forms and is often planned months in advance. In Southern Germany, where Carnival is called Fasching, there are fancy dress balls and masked processions. In Mexico and Brazil there are colourful floats with real actors performing plays about bandits and the triumph of good over evil.

In the South of France a King of the Carnival leads the merry-making with a court of clowns, and there are floats filled with beautiful flowers. In Spain, thousands of people walk in procession at fiesta time. Castanets and guitars accompany dancing in the street.

Carnival is equally popular in the West Indies. Here the music of steel bands fills the air and everyone makes lovely elaborate costumes to wear.

In Germany doughnuts and pretzels are eaten at Carnival time. Pretzels are doughnuts which have been shaped into a long roll. They are then folded to make a bun with three holes in it.

The very first pretzels are said to have been invented by a baker who lived at the foot of the Alps. He was thrown into prison because he had been supplying bad bread. Only on one condition would he be freed – if he could bake something through which the sun would shine three times. And so after lots of thought and many sleepless nights he came up with the pretzel!

Pretzels

Traditionally pretzels are deep fried but they are just as good baked in the oven.

Ingredients

1¼ teaspoons dried yeast
25 g sugar
125 ml lukewarm milk
225 g plain flour
pinch salt

¼ teaspoon ground cinnamon
50 g melted butter
1 egg, beaten
cooking oil

Equipment

measuring jug
sieve

mixing bowl
baking sheet

Method

1 Mix the dried yeast and sugar with the milk and leave to stand in a warm place for 10 minutes until the milk looks a little frothy.
2 Sift the flour, salt, and cinnamon into a bowl and make a well in the centre.
3 Pour on the yeast and sugar mixture, and add the butter and half the beaten egg. Mix to a smooth dough with your hands and knead lightly for 3–4 minutes.
4 Cover and leave to stand for 20 minutes.
5 With floured hands divide the mixture in six small portions.
6 Roll each portion into a sausage shape about 35 cm long.
7 Shape as shown opposite.
8 Leave to stand on a floured baking tray for a further 20 minutes.
   Brush with the remaining beaten egg.
   Bake at 220°C/425°F/Gas 7 for 10 minutes.

Makes 8.

Note: if you can find Dried Active Yeast with Vitamin C omit stages 1 and 4, and mix the yeast in with the flour. Then add the milk along with the butter and egg at stage 3.

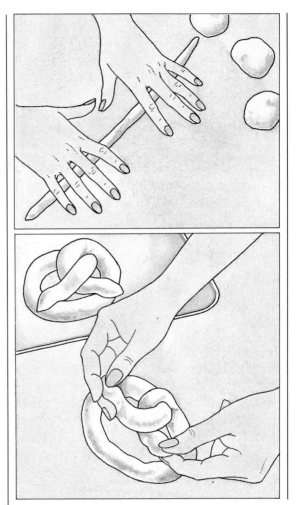

Shrove Tuesday

The forty days before the Christian festival of Easter are known as Lent. Their origin lies in the forty days which, the Bible tells us, Jesus Christ spent praying in the wilderness before beginning to teach. At the end of these forty days the Devil came to tempt Jesus with food and worldly glory. But Jesus refused all the Devil's temptations, telling him to go away.

Lent is a time when Christians prepare for Easter. It begins on Ash Wednesday. In the past everyone tried to make a good start by confessing their sins to a priest the day before. They hoped to have their sins forgiven. Another word for forgiven is "shriven", and so that is why the day came to be called Shrove Tuesday.

During Lent everyone had to live more simply. Today some people still try to give up things which they really enjoy. But in the Middle Ages there was no choice. Everyone had to go without eating meat, eggs, and lard.

Housewives did their best to use up these foods before Lent started. One dish they made was pancakes. In Scotland it was oatcakes, which are often called bannocks.

In some places, like Olney in Buckinghamshire, the "Pancake" bell is still rung to remind people to come to church to confess their sins. A five hundred-year-old Pancake Race is run in the same town.

The story is told that in 1445 a housewife was busy cooking the family pancakes when she heard the "Pancake" bell. So, not wanting to be late, she rushed off down the village street still clutching her frying pan and wearing her apron.

In France, Shrove Tuesday is called "Mardi Gras" which means Greasy Tuesday, again referring to the fact that all the grease and fat had to be used up. All over France school children enjoy making and eating crêpes, the French name for pancakes.

At Westminster School in London, the cook tosses an extra large pancake over a bar 4.8 metres above the ground, which separates the Upper and Lower schools. The boys all scramble for bits of the pancake and the one who emerges with the largest piece wins a cash prize.

As well as fasting and doing without, Lent was a time for prayer and thought. So Shrove Tuesday was also used to let off steam. People took part in energetic competitions and games. This is probably why there are so many traditional football matches played on that day.

Pancakes

Pancakes are traditionally served sprinkled with lemon juice and sugar.

Ingredients
100 g plain flour
pinch salt
1 egg
250 ml milk
cooking oil

Equipment
mixing bowl
wooden spoon
heavy frying pan
tablespoon
fish slice
measuring jug

Method

1 Sift the flour and salt into a bowl.
2 Make a well in the centre and add the egg and half the milk.
Stir the mixture, gradually drawing in the flour from the sides of the bowl.
3 When all the flour has been mixed in, beat very well with a wooden spoon and add the rest of the milk.
4 Heat a very little oil in a heavy frying pan.
5 Stir the batter and put 2–3 tablespoons into the pan.
Tip the pan so the batter completely covers the base.
6 Cook for about a minute until the pancake is set and golden underneath.
7 Shake the pan to loosen the pancake and turn over.
Cook the second side for another minute or so.
8 Continue until all the batter is used up.

Makes 8–10.

Suggested fillings

Sweet
Apple sauce (see page 61) and yogurt
Chopped fresh oranges and raisins
Chopped hazelnuts and chocolate sauce

Savoury
Sloppy Joe filling (see page 37)

Holi

A traditional painting of Holi celebrations

Holi is the Hindu festival which celebrates the end of winter and the arrival of spring. Like the other spring festivals it falls some time during late February and early March.

Bonfires are lit, and people burn an image of the legendary demon Holika as a symbol that good has once again defeated evil. Rubbish is burnt on the bonfires to show that past wrong doing is forgiven. People also roast grain, such as barley, and coconuts in the fire. Some is offered in thanks to the fire, and the rest is eaten as holy food.

Holi is a happy friendly time. Everyone, rich or poor, joins in the festivities. It is known as the festival of colour in honour of the spring flowers. In India people buy red powder and coloured water to throw over each other and everyone wears bright colours. In some parts, there are processions with statues of the Hindu Gods being carried through the streets.

The Hindu god, Lord Krishna, is particularly honoured at this time and his love for a girl called Radha is celebrated. The most interesting Holi celebration takes place at Barsana, the legendary home town of Radha. The woman of Barsana challenge the men of Nandagon, Lord Krishna's home, to throw colour on them. The men accept this challenge the next day.

In the Punjab towns of Northern India, a sect of the Sikh community observes Hola Mohalla which is similar to Holi. They stage mock battles with ancient weapons and horse riding and athletics competitions. Children's parties are held with lots of fun and special foods.

In India, Holi is a public festival celebrated in the open air, but in Britain Hindus do not throw coloured water in the street. So the festival is held indoors, and there are private parties with singing and dancing and feasting.

Merchant selling coloured powder

Spiced Vegetable Croquettes

Many Hindus avoid eating meat. Here is a recipe for delicious spiced croquettes which do not use meat but which do use toasted cereals as a coating. Serve with plain yogurt.

Ingredients

1 tablespoon cooking oil	40 g rolled oats
½ teaspoon whole cumin seeds	1 carrot, peeled
1 onion, finely chopped	1 medium potato, peeled
1 × 213 g can butter beans, well drained	1 teaspoon garam masala
	salt and pepper
	1 egg, beaten

Equipment

grill pan	fork
frying pan	basin
baking tray	grater
wooden spoon	

Method

1 Set the oven to 190°C/375°F/Gas 5 and grease the baking tray.

2 Sprinkle the rolled oats into the base of the grill pan and toast under the grill, shaking the tray from time to time. The oats will take about 1–1½ minutes to brown.
Leave on one side to cool.

3 Heat the oil in a frying pan.
Add the cumin seeds and stir.
After about a minute the seeds will begin to pop.

4 Add the onions and fry for 3–4 minutes until lightly browned.
Leave on one side.

5 Mash the butter beans with a fork in a large basin.
Stir in the fried onions.

6 Grate the carrot and potato and squeeze out any liquid.

7 Add these vegetables to the butter bean and onion mixture.
Stir in the garam masala and seasoning.
(See page 23)

8 Divide the mixture into four quarters and shape into flat croquettes.

9 Wash and dry your hands.
Dip each croquette in egg and then sprinkle each side with the toasted oats.
Place on the greased baking tray.

10 Bake the croquettes for 30–35 minutes.

Serves 2.

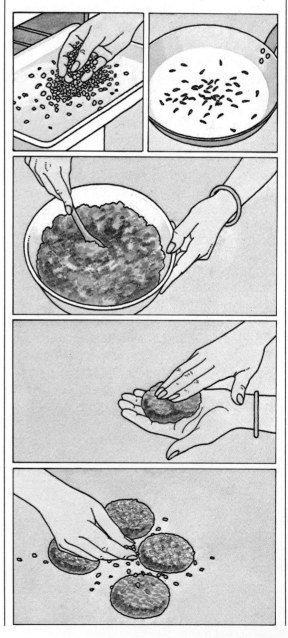

Mothering Sunday

This falls on the fourth Sunday in Lent. Before the Reformation, when the Church of England broke away from the Catholic Church in Rome, it was the one day during Lent when feasting and games were allowed. Perhaps this is why it used to be known as Refreshment Sunday.

It is now known as Mothering Sunday. This is because people who lived in places which were too poor or too small to have a church of their own would travel to the Mother or parish church on this Sunday of Lent.

In later centuries, young people started to work away from home as servants or apprentices. It became the custom for them to be given the day off on this particular Sunday so that they could visit their parents.

Often the cooks in the great houses would bake cakes for the other servants to take home as presents. Bunches of flowers might be picked for Mother on the way home. Today children who are away from home still send flowers and cards. In America the Senate and the House of Representatives officially named the day "Mother's Day".

The traditional cake for Mothering Sunday is a Simnel Cake. One kind is the Bury Simnel which is a flat cake filled with currants and almonds. The other is the Shrewsbury Simnel which is a dark rich fruit cake with a hard crown of almond paste. Nowadays the cake is often served at Easter and it is topped with balls of almond paste representing the apostles.

There are a number of different stories told about the beginnings of the name "Simnel Cake". The cakes probably take their name from the very fine flour with which the cakes were made. It was called "Simila".

More romantic is the tale which claims that the cake is named after Lambert Simnel, who claimed he was heir to the throne of Henry VII and whose father was a baker. But in fact Simnel cakes were well known before then.

A third story tells of a man named Simon and his wife Nell who quarrelled about the best way to cook the cake. In the end they compromised and the cake became known as a combination of both their names.

Mothering Sunday Buns

These little buns are made with raisins and can be decorated with butter icing and tiny marzipan balls to make attractive Mother's Day presents. They are much easier to make than the larger Simnel cake in the picture below. But they are every bit as delicious. They are just right for a Mothering Sunday tea.

Ingredients

50 g butter or margarine, softened	50 g plain flour
50 g sugar	½ teaspoon baking powder
1 egg, beaten	40 g raisins

Topping:

50 g butter	125 g icing sugar
grated lemon rind	50 g marzipan or almond paste
1 teaspoon lemon juice	

Equipment

mixing bowl	paper bun cases
wooden spoon	baking tray
tablespoon	basin
teaspoon	knife

Method

1 Place the butter and sugar in a bowl and beat with a wooden spoon until light and fluffy.
2 Add the beaten egg a little at a time (adding a little flour if the mixture shows signs of separating).
3 Fold in the flour, baking powder, and raisins with a tablespoon.
4 Drop spoonfuls of the mixture into paper bun cases.
   Place on a baking tray and bake at 180°C/350°F/Gas 4 for 15–20 minutes.
   Leave to cool on a wire rack.
5 To make the topping, cream the butter in a basin and add the lemon rind and juice and half the icing sugar.
   Carefully beat together.
6 Add the remaining sugar and mix to a smooth paste.
7 Break small pieces off the marzipan and roll into very small balls.
8 Spread a little of the lemon butter icing over each bun and place a few of the marzipan balls on top.

Makes 10–12.

Baisakhi Day

Sikh riding through Old Delhi

Baisakhi Day, which falls in April, is one of the most important days in the Sikh calendar. It celebrates the start, in 1699, of what is known as the Pure Sikh Community, and it is also the Sikh New Year.

The Sikh religion was founded by a man called Nanak who was born in 1469 in Lahore, in what is now Pakistan. When he was still very young Nanak rejected the Hindu ceremonies. He taught that there was just one God who is worshipped by all the different faiths.

Nanak believed that God is present in everyone and everything. He did not think that priests or ritual ceremonies were necessary for people to find their way to God. He thought that quiet prayer and a good moral life were more likely to succeed.

Ten leaders, or gurus, followed Nanak. One of them, Guru Arjun, collected all the hymns and prayers of the Sikh gurus who had preceded him, and added some Muslim and Hindu writings as well. This became the Adi Granth or Sikh "Bible".

Guru Gobind Singh was the tenth and last Guru. He decided to form a select group of Sikhs who would live up to and defend all the teaching of the faith. He chose the men by holding up a sword and calling on all true Sikhs to allow him to cut off their heads as a sign of their faith. No one moved. He asked three times and at the third attempt one Sikh stood up.

Guru Gobind took this man away and reappeared with a sword dripping in blood. He asked again for a true Sikh to offer his life. One man reluctantly came forward and was also taken away. Guru Gobind repeated his request five times. Then, before the remaining crowd, he brought out all five men alive and unhurt.

These men, because of their faith and courage were to be the core of the Pure Sikhs. They were "baptized" by the sword and took the name of "Singh" or lion.

They swore to wear long hair, a comb, and trousers. They also wear a fine steel bracelet as a sign of spiritual allegiance and a steel dagger for the defence of the faith.

Since then Sikhs have been baptized into the faith on this day of the year. Everyone goes to the Sikh temple, or Gurdwara. New clothes are worn and presents of turbans are given.

Spicy Fried Chicken

Although Sikhs do not have strict food laws, many are vegetarians. Often, on festival days, the whole family will eat a vegetarian meal at the communal canteen in their temple. But many Sikhs do eat meat. This recipe is for a typical spicy Sikh meal.

Ingredients
2 chicken breasts, boned and skinned *or* the meat from 3 or 4 thigh joints
1 onion, sliced
½ clove garlic, chopped
2½ cm piece fresh root ginger, chopped

juice of 1 lemon
1 tablespoon vegetable oil
1 teaspoon ground coriander
½ teaspoon ground cumin
pinch chilli powder or garam masala
salt

Equipment
bowl
knife
deep frying pan
wooden spoon

Method

1 Cut the meat into small pieces and cover with lemon juice.
   Leave to stand for a while.
2 Fry the onion, clove of garlic, and ginger in cooking oil for 2–3 minutes, stirring all the time.
3 When the onion begins to turn golden add the pieces of chicken.
   Discard the lemon juice.
4 Fry the chicken with the vegetables for 10 minutes, turning from time to time.
5 When the chicken is golden in colour add all the remaining ingredients.
   Keep tossing and frying the mixture for a further 10 minutes.
6 Serve hot with boiled rice (see page 9).

Serves 2.

Key to spices:
	A	ALLSPICE OR PIMENTO	
B	CUMIN		
C	CINNAMON	**D**	TURMERIC
E	GINGER	**F**	BLACK PEPPER	**G**	CARDAMOM
H	NUTMEG	**I**	CHILLI	**J**	CORIANDER

Garam Masala

This is a mixture of different spices which Indians use to flavour their dishes. It can be made up in advance and stored in an air-tight jar. If you like a hotter dish, simply add chilli powder to the ingredients. You can also buy the mixture ready made.

Ingredients
1 tablespoon ground coriander
1 tablespoon ground cumin
1 teaspoon ground cardamom

½ teaspoon ground cloves
½ teaspoon ground black pepper

Equipment
small glass jar
tablespoon
teaspoon

Method

Spoon all the ingredients into the jar.
Stir with a spoon.
Cover with a lid and shake well.

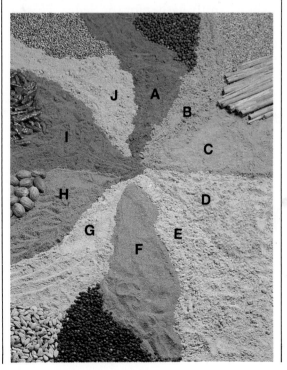

Passover

This Jewish holiday is one of the world's oldest festivals. It existed long before the first Easter. In fact Jesus Christ himself celebrated Passover at His "Last Supper" just before he was crucified.

It is celebrated in memory of the Exodus of the Jews from Egypt. A very long time ago, about 1250 BC, the Jews or Hebrews were slaves to the Pharaoh or King of Egypt. With God's help, Moses led them to freedom in their Promised Land. The holiday is called Passover because God passed over the Jewish houses when he slew the first born children of Egypt. The Jewish children were protected by lambs' blood which had been smeared on the doors of their homes.

Passover lasts for a week and there are special services on the first and last days. However, the festival is really a family festival and is celebrated in the home. On the first night of Passover, and sometimes on the first and second nights, the whole family gather for the Seder. This is when the family comes together for a history lesson and service, to remember the Exodus from Egypt.

In the centre of the table is a plate containing a number of symbolic foods. These are there to remind the Jews of the details of the story. There is a lamb bone as a reminder of the lambs' blood. Parsley is a reminder of spring, and, before it is eaten, it is dipped in salt water.

The salt water represents the tears of the slaves in Egypt and the Red Sea which parted to allow the Jews to escape. There are bitter herbs to make tears come to the eyes, again a reminder of the slave's tears. However, these are dipped in a sweet paste called haroset before being eaten. This paste represents the mortar the slaves used in buildings. The bitter herbs and the sweet paste are together a reminder of a bitter beginning and a sweet or happy ending.

During the Seder the youngest child present asks special questions beginning with "Why is this night different from any other night?" As the answers are given the story unfolds. The symbolic food is eaten or displayed at the appropriate places in the story.

During the whole week of Passover, many Jews do not eat leavened bread. This is because on the day the Jews left Egypt there wasn't time to let the dough rise, and everyone had to eat quickly baked unleavened bread. Today Matzoth, rather like dry water biscuits, are eaten during Passover.

Haroset

This recipe is typical of the haroset served in British and American Jewish homes. Each family has its own traditional recipe. Some families may add chopped raisins and dates.

Ingredients

3 apples	1 teaspoon water
50 g flaked or chopped almonds	¼ teaspoon cinnamon
1 tablespoon sugar	

Equipment

knife
food processor or blender
basin

Method

1 Peel and core the apples and cut into chunks.
2 Place all the ingredients in a food processor or blender and blend to a paste. If you do not have any electrical equipment, chop all the ingredients as finely as possible and mix well together.
3 Serve with Matzoth.

Egyptian Haroset

This version comes from an Egyptian family.

Ingredients

100 g raisins, chopped	100 ml water
50 g stoned dates, chopped	40 g brown sugar
	15 g walnuts, finely chopped

Equipment

kitchen knife	small saucepan
basin	bowl

Method

1 Place the raisins and dates in a basin, cover with water, and leave to stand for 20–30 minutes.
2 Transfer the fruit and water to a small saucepan, and add the sugar.
   Bring to the boil and simmer over a low heat until all the liquid has disappeared, about 10–15 minutes.
   Stir from time to time.
3 Spoon into a small bowl and when cool sprinkle with the walnuts.

Serve with Matzoth.

Easter

Easter or Holy Week really starts on the Thursday before Easter. This is called Maundy Thursday and church services remember the Last Supper which Jesus had with the twelve apostles. It became the custom, on this day, to give money and presents to the poor and needy. The Queen still gives a purse of specially minted silver Maundy pennies to a group of selected pensioners and poor people.

Good Friday remembers the day on which Jesus was crucified and it used to be called "God's Friday". It is a sad time when Christians go to church or stay quietly at home.

It is also the traditional day for eating Hot Cross buns. The history of these buns goes back to Roman times when little buns were made to welcome the Spring. With the coming of Christianity, a cross was drawn on the top of the buns.

According to tradition, a Hot Cross bun made on Good Friday morning will not go bad or mouldy if stored in the right kind of dry conditions.

In the past it was not unusual to see them after Easter, strung up from the kitchen rafters. They were thought to be very lucky and to have the ability to cure various common illnesses.

Easter Sunday is the greatest feast of the Christian year. It marks the end of Lent, and the sadness of Good Friday is over. Easter is always on the Sunday following the first full moon appearing on or after 21st March.

The Bible tells how Jesus was buried in a cave after the crucifixion and the entrance was blocked with a heavy rock. When his mother and friends came to the tomb they found that the rock had been rolled away and the tomb was empty. Christians believe that he had risen from the dead. The message of Easter is that death is not the end of life. It is the beginning of a new kind of life.

Eggs have always been regarded as symbols of new life. Thus eggs have come to be associated with the joy of the Resurrection. As well as chocolate Easter eggs and painted hard-boiled eggs, there are many other customs which still survive such as egg rolling. Two places where egg rolling takes place are Avenham Park, Preston, and the lawn of the White House in Washington USA.

Pace Eggs

In places as far apart as the Lake District in England and the Ukraine in Russia, bowls of brightly coloured and decorated eggs are piled into baskets and offered to Easter guests.

Dyed eggs

Eggs can be dyed as they are cooked. Use 20 drops of red, blue, green, or yellow food colours and one teaspoon of vinegar to every 300 ml of boiling water. Natural dyes which can also be used are beetroot, onion skins, and coffee grounds.

Patterns

Patterns can be made on the eggs by carefully drawing on the shells with a waxed pen. This probably is best done when the eggs have first been cooked in plain water. Boil again in the water with the dye and the wax will keep the pattern clear of dye.

Painted eggs

Any kind of pattern, funny face, or pictures can be drawn on eggs which have been hard-boiled and left to cool. Use paint brushes and food colours or coloured pentel pens.

Method

1 Place the water in an old saucepan, add the food colour or a handful of the natural dyeing ingredients, and bring to the boil.
2 Pierce the end of the eggs with an egg piercer to stop them cracking.
   Carefully lower into the water with a spoon.
3 Boil for 12 minutes and remove from the water. Leave to cool.
4 Rub with a little olive oil or candle wax to give a bright shine.

Vesak

that he should share his new knowledge with other people. So he travelled all over Northern India preaching.

The Buddha's teaching was not concerned with God but with how people can live in harmony without misery. He said that human wants and desires were the basis of all suffering. If people gave up their desires they would no longer suffer.

At Vesak, Buddhists gather in the temple and the statue of the Buddha is decorated with flowers. A monk or leader talks about the Buddha's enlightenment and his teachings. People also decorate their homes with garlands and candles, and give presents.

In the East gifts of money and food are secretly left on the door steps of the poor, and captured birds are set free in memory of the Buddha's concern for mankind.

Decorated statue of the Buddha (left)
Palace and Buddhist temple in Thailand (below)

For Buddhists the festival of Vesak is the most important religious festival of the year. It celebrates the life of the Buddha and takes place on, or near to, the May full moon.

Buddha means "awakened one" or a person who has gained complete wisdom and understanding of the world. People gave this name to an Indian prince who lived more than 2500 years ago.

His name was Siddhartha Gautama and, when he was 29, he left the luxurious palace in which he lived, to begin a life of fasting and meditation. He listened to all the Hindu priests but did not like their teachings.

Then one day as he was sitting beneath a tree, enlightenment or complete understanding of life came to him. He decided

Vegetable Koftas in Curry Sauce

Strict Buddhists are vegetarian but their food varies from country to country. This recipe comes from Northern India where the Buddha wandered and taught the people.

Ingredients

250 g carrots
175 g canned chick-peas, well drained
40 g semolina
1 clove garlic, chopped
1 teaspoon grated fresh root ginger

1 large onion
1 teaspoon ground coriander
½ teaspoon ground turmeric
salt and pepper
flour

Curry Sauce

1 × 418 g can tomatoes
1 onion
2 teaspoons garam masala (page 23)
salt

2 teaspoons ground cumin
1 teaspoon freshly chopped mint
pinch cayenne pepper

Equipment

saucepans with lids
kitchen knife
grater
teaspoon

tablespoon
sieve
deep frying pan

Method

1 Peel and slice the carrots.
Place in a pan and cover with water.
Bring to the boil, cover, and simmer for 15 minutes until cooked.
2 Start on the sauce now.
Empty the contents of the can of tomatoes into a saucepan.
Add all the other sauce ingredients and bring to the boil.
3 Simmer the sauce for 15 minutes.
Rub through a sieve and pour into a deep frying pan.
4 Drain the carrots well and mash coarsely with the chick-peas.
Stir in the semolina.
5 Grate the onions on the coarse grater, and squeeze as dry as possible.
Add to the carrot mixture with the garlic, ginger, spices, and seasoning.
Mix well together.
6 Flour your hands and shape the mixture into 16 small balls the size of walnuts.
7 Place the vegetable balls in the curry sauce, and bring to the boil.
Simmer gently for 10 minutes until they are cooked through.

Serve with rice or pitta bread, and salad.

Serves 4.

Whitsuntide

Young children ready to take part in a Whit Walk

Forty days after Easter comes Ascension Thursday, when Christians remember how Jesus Christ went up to Heaven. After his crucifixion, Jesus rose from the dead on Easter Sunday. He then spent forty days visiting his apostles and preparing them for their missions to spread His teachings throughout the world.

Whitsuntide comes ten days after Ascension Thursday. At one time Whit Sunday was known as "White Sunday" as many people were baptized on that day. They all wore white clothes for the happy occasion.

The first Whit Sunday is sometimes called the birthday of the Christian Church. This is because Jesus brought the Holy Spirit of God to His apostles on that day to give them the strength to go out and preach. His apostles were then able to spread the teachings of Jesus far and wide.

In the past most parishes used to hold a church feast at Whitsuntide. It was a social occasion for the parishioners but it was also used to raise money for the church.

There were games, competitions, and singing and dancing. Sometimes there were performances of "mystery plays". The plays are based on the Bible stories. They are not called "mystery" plays because they are religious or mysterious, but because they used to be performed by craftsmen. In the past a craft was also called a "mystery".

In Lancashire and Greater Manchester there are church processions of local people dressed in their best clothes. These are called the Whit Walks and the people are demonstrating their faith.

Whitsun Lamb Roast

At Kingsteignton in Devon a whole lamb is roasted on a spit. The villagers eat it after taking part in games and dancing. This feast is held in memory of the time when the village stream ran dry. Everyone prayed for the water to start flowing again and it did. The village sacrificed a lamb in thanks. Here is a simple recipe for roast breast of lamb. Serve with fresh mint sauce.

Ingredients
1 boned breast of
   lamb
sprigs of fresh mint,
   finely chopped
salt and pepper

Equipment
knife
string
roasting tray

Method

1 Set the oven to 190°C/375°F/Gas 5.
2 Cut off as much fat as you can from the meat and then remove any tough skin or membrane from each side of the breast. This stops the joint from being stringy.
3 Lay the breast skinside down on a board. Sprinkle with chopped mint and salt and pepper.
4 Roll up the breast and secure it with string.
5 Place the lamb in a roasting tin and roast for one hour.
   Cut into slices to serve.

Serves 2 or 3.

Fresh Mint Sauce

Ingredients
1 small bunch fresh   a little freshly ground
   mint   black pepper
juice of 1 lemon

Equipment
knife or parsley mill   sieve
sauceboat   spoon

Method

1 Chop the mint very finely and place it in a small sauceboat.
2 Squeeze the lemon, and strain the juice over the mint.
   Stir once and serve with the lamb.

Serves 4.

Shavuot

Decorating the synagogue for Shavuot

This Jewish festival is also called the Feast of Weeks or Pentecost. It falls exactly fifty days after Passover. Hence the name "Pentecost" which means fiftieth.

It usually falls in May or early June. At first the festival marked the end of the barley harvest, and the first fruits of the harvest were offered to God in the Temple. Later it also came to celebrate the giving of the Ten Commandments to Moses on Mount Sinai.

The synagogue is decorated with flowers and a special service is held. The Bible story of Ruth is often read. It is about a non-Jewish girl who was the ancestor of the Jewish King David.

Dairy foods are usually eaten in Jewish homes at Shavuot. In some families the first meal of the day will be based on milk

and cheese and cream. The second meal may use meat.

Dairy foods have always been plentiful at this time of the year. Goats, sheep, and cows are all able to graze on the new spring grass and they therefore produce more milk.

However, some experts suggest that the Israelites fasted and ate nothing before they went to Mount Sinai to receive the Ten Commandments. They were very hungry when they returned and immediately drank milk, instead of taking time to prepare and cook a meal with meat.

Another reason suggested for eating cheese at this time may be that by the time the Israelites returned to camp, their milk had turned sour and separated. This is the first step in cheese-making.

Cheesecake

This is a family recipe from Israel.

Ingredients

8 digestive biscuits
60 g butter or
  margarine
225 g cream cheese
100 g sugar
4 eggs, separated

juice of ½ lemon
50 g plain flour
½ teaspoon baking
  powder
½ teaspoon salt

Equipment

polythene bag
rolling pin
small saucepan
25 cm loose-based
  cake tin

bowl
wooden spoon
teaspoon
whisk
tablespoon

Method

1　Set the oven to 180°C/350°F/Gas 4.
2　Place the digestive biscuits in a polythene bag and crush with a rolling pin.
Empty the crumbs into a basin.
3　Melt the butter and pour over the biscuit crumbs.
Mix well together and press well into the base of 23 cm cake tin.
4　Beat the cream cheese with two tablespoons of sugar, egg yolks, and lemon juice.
Mix in the flour, baking powder, and salt.
5　Whisk the egg whites until they are very stiff.
Gradually whisk in the remaining sugar.
6　Gently fold this mixture into the cheese mixture.
7　Pour over the biscuit base in the cake tin.
8　Bake for 50–55 minutes until the cake is well risen and brown on top.
9　Leave to cool before removing the cheesecake from the cake tin.

Serves 6–8.

Dragon Boat Festival

Dragon Boat race in Hong Kong

The Chinese Dragon Boat Festival falls on the fifth day of the fifth month in the Chinese lunar calendar. This is usually somewhere around Midsummer's Day.

In China local towns and villages compete in boat races. The boats are rowing boats which often have a dragon head carved on the front. Chinese people, unlike Westerners, row facing the way they are going.

Some experts believe that the festival began as an attempt to keep away the powers of evil that would bring the winter. Others say that the dragon boats were thought to be magic and to bring rain. The dragon was a water God, and rain was caused by dragons fighting in the clouds. Summer is the time when rain is needed for growing crops, so they tried to bring rain by holding dragon fights between the boats.

However, the story believed by most Chinese people concerns the poet Qu Yuan. In some parts, the festival is known as Poet's Day. Qu Yuan lived about 300 BC. He was a wise counsellor and a poet. One day his wise advice was rejected by the leaders of China. So, he threw himself into the water to protest against the bad government of his country.

People rushed in boats to save him but could not do so. The people also threw cooked rice into the water to stop the water animals and fish eating his body. Later his ghost appeared to some fishermen. He told them to parcel up rice in silk and tie the parcels with coloured threads as their protection against the water spirits.

Since then people have remembered the attempt to rescue Qu Yuan with the boat races. They also eat rice dumplings which have been wrapped in leaves and tied with raffia.

Steamed Rice Dumplings

These little steamed rice cakes can be eaten hot or cold. In China they are wrapped in coloured paper and ribbon, and given as gifts.

If you don't have a Chinese grocer anywhere near and cannot get glutinous rice, use pudding rice instead.

Ingredients

100 g glutinous rice
water
50 g cooked chicken
    meat

1 hard-boiled egg
25 g frozen peas,
    thawed
salt and pepper

Equipment

pudding basin
grinder
mixing bowl

spoon
egg poacher

Method

1 Leave the rice to soak in cold water overnight.
2 Next day drain very well and grind it in a grinder or food processor.
3 Chop the chicken and hard-boiled egg very finely and add to the rice with the peas, salt, and pepper.
   Mix well together.
4 Form the mixture into 8 small cakes by squeezing it in your hands.
5 Place each cake in the cups of the egg poacher.
   Fill the base with water.
6 Poach the cakes for 10–12 minutes until set.

Makes 8.

Variation

Sweet dumplings can be made by leaving out the chicken and peas from the above recipe.

Add instead 25 g each of sugar, chopped nuts, raisins, and chopped dates.

American Independence Day

The Boston Tea Party

The fourth of July is the day on which the United States of America celebrates its independence. It was on this day in 1776 that the English colonists in America issued a "Declaration of Independence".

The first English people went to settle in America in 1620. As time went by, the grandchildren and great grandchildren of those first colonists began to think of America as their home and of England only as a distant mother-country.

But, in England, the government continued to think of the people in North America as colonists who should still send back money to England to pay the taxes. Gradually the colonists began to resent having to send back their hard-earned money to England. They did not believe they were getting anything back for the taxes they paid.

One of the taxes the colonists disliked the most was the duty they had to pay on imports of tea. In 1773, some of them dressed up as local Red Indians and threw about three hundred chests of tea from three tea ships into Boston harbour. This protest became known as the Boston Tea Party. It showed how strongly the American settlers felt about getting the right to govern themselves.

The settlers said that it was unfair that they should pay taxes when they were not allowed to elect Members of Parliament to represent them. Their slogan became "no taxation without representation". However, the British Parliament did not agree, and the War of American Independence began in 1775. The war lasted for eight years. In the end the colonists won, and America became an independent nation.

When the Declaration of Independence was signed in 1776 the Liberty Bell was rung. This is a famous bell which hangs in Philadelphia. On it are inscribed the words, "Proclaim liberty throughout the land, unto all the inhabitants thereof." It is still rung every 4th July.

Independence Day in America is a public holiday. There is no school and families celebrate together. Streets are hung with flags and decorations, and there are pageants and parades with fireworks in the evening.

Sloppy Joes

This is a kind of runny hamburger which American children like to have as a change from the regular variety. They are served in sesame buns, with relishes and ketchup on the side.

Ingredients

1 medium onion, peeled
1 small green pepper, seeded
350 g lean beef, minced
50 g mushrooms
salt and pepper
2 teaspoons tomato ketchup
4 sesame buns
lettuce leaves

Equipment

kitchen knife
non-stick saucepan
wooden spoon
teaspoon

Method

1 Very finely chop the onion, green pepper, and mushrooms.
2 Dry fry the minced beef to release the fat and pour off any excess.
3 Add the chopped vegetables to the pan with the seasoning and tomato ketchup. Bring to the boil.
Reduce the heat and simmer for 15–20 minutes.
4 Cut the tops off the buns and scoop out a little of the dough.
Fill each bun with some of the meat mixture.
Top with a lettuce leaf and your favourite relish.
Cover with the top of the bun.

Makes 4.

Barbecued Hamburgers

In America barbecues are a favourite form of entertainment for Independence Day. Here is a recipe for Barbecued Hamburgers which can be cooked over a barbecue or under a grill.

Ingredients

450g lean beef, minced
1 teaspoon tomato ketchup
½ teaspoon Worcestershire Sauce
salt and pepper

Equipment

bowl
fork

Method

1 Place all the ingredients in a bowl and mix very well with a fork.
2 Divide the mixture into 4 portions.
Shape each portion into a hamburger with your hands, and squeeze gently to make the meat stick together.
3 Grill for about 4–6 minutes each side.

Makes 4.

Bastille Day

Marie Antoinette

This French holiday celebrates freedom from a very unfair government within the people's own country. In eighteenth-century France the peasants were starving, but they were still very heavily taxed. But at the same time the nobles were living in great luxury.

A request to help the poor was turned down by the King, Louis XVI. His wife, Marie Antoinette, when told that there was not even enough bread to eat, is supposed to have said, "Let them eat cake."

At that time the main prison in France was called the Bastille and it was a grim symbol of royal tyranny. Anyone could be placed there simply on the word of the king.

When the French Revolution began in 1789, one of the first targets of the revolutionaries was the Bastille. A mob of Parisian citizens stormed the prison on 14th July. The governor of the prison was killed, and the prisoners were carried off in triumph.

Soon afterwards the prison was pulled down. All that can now be seen is the shape of the ancient fortress in the line of the paving stones in the Bastille Square.

Today, 14th July is a national holiday in France. Celebrations usually begin the evening before, with processions and fireworks. Families gather together, and most French people will cook a special meal or the family will all go out to their local restaurants to celebrate.

Soldiers of the French Revolution executing Louis XVI

Saveloy and Hot Potato Salad

This dish comes from the region near Lyon in the Rhône valley in South-East France. It is often served as a starter to the main meal. However, it also makes a good lunch or supper dish served with grated carrot salad.

Ingredients

450 g small red-skinned potatoes
175 g saveloy sausages
1 tablespoon cooking oil
1 tablespoon red or white wine vinegar
salt and freshly ground black pepper
lettuce leaves, well washed
1 tablespoon freshly chopped chives
3 tablespoons olive oil

Equipment

saucepan
knife
frying pan
jam jar
mixing bowl
serving bowl

Method

1 Scrub the potatoes clean and place them in a saucepan.
   Cover with water and bring to the boil. Reduce heat and simmer for 15–20 minutes, depending on the size of the potatoes, until tender.
2 Meanwhile, remove any skin from the saveloys and slice or cut into cubes.
3 Heat the oil in a frying pan and fry the saveloys until crisp and brown on each side.
   Keep warm on one side.
4 Pour the olive oil and vinegar into a jam jar Add the salt and pepper and cover with a lid.
   Shake well together.
   Pour into a bowl.
5 Drain the potatoes well and skin.
   Cut into halves or quarters, and drop into the oil and vinegar mixture.
6 Shake the lettuce to remove any excess water.
   Use to line the serving bowl.
7 Spoon on the potatoes and their dressing and top with the fried sausage.

Serves 4 as a starter, and 2 as a main course.

Raksha Bandhan and Janam Ashtami

A scene from the life of Krishna

The family is very important to Hindus and Raksha Bandhan is a family celebration for brothers and sisters. It falls on the day of the full moon in the Hindu month of Shravana. This is usually at the end of July or in August.

Raksha Bandhan, or Rakhi, actually means a tie. Not the kind of tie you put round your neck, but the bond between brothers and sisters. The festival is based on an old legend which tells how the God Indra was protected from demons by a silk bracelet called a rakhi which was given to him by his wife.

On Raksha Bandhan day, sisters make a silk bracelet of red and gold thread which they tie to their brothers' wrists. They also mark their brothers foreheads with vermilion powder.

The gift of the bracelet shows the sister's love for her brother. By wearing the bracelet, the brother promises to protect her for ever. The vermilion powder is used as a symbol of success and victory. Very often the brother will give his sister a present in return.

Also in August is the Janam Ashtami. This Hindu festival celebrates the birth of the god-hero Krishna. He is very important to Hindus, for he is believed to have been the God Vishnu in human form. Many Hindus watch through the night in the Temples, and scenes from Krishna's life are acted out.

Indian Banana Fudge

Hindus often give presents of sweetmeats at their special festivals. They are often eaten in the temples during the night-long watch at Janam Ashtami. This, and the next recipe, comes from Southern India where bananas and coconuts are plentiful.

Ingredients

1 large banana
3 cardamom pods
25 g butter or
    margarine
50 g semolina
50 g ground almonds
50 g brown sugar
4 tablespoons water

Equipment

plate
fork
small saucepan
wooden spoon
shallow tin
rolling pin

Method

1 Mash the banana with a fork and keep on one side.
2 Remove the seeds from the cardamom pods and crush between sheets of paper or polythene with a rolling pin, or grind in a pestle and mortar.
    Add to the bananas.
3 Melt the butter in a saucepan and gently fry the semolina until it turns golden in colour.
4 Stir in the bananas, ground almonds, sugar, and water.
5 Bring to the boil and cook, stirring all the time, until the mixture comes away from the sides of the pan.
6 Spoon into a shallow greased tin and place in the fridge to set.
    Cut into small squares.

Makes 12–14 squares.

Coconut Barfi

Ingredients

175 g can evaporated
    milk
75 g desiccated
    coconut
100 g golden
    granulated sugar

Equipment

saucepan
wooden spoon

Method

1 Pour the contents of the can of milk into the saucepan.
    Add the sugar and heat gently, stirring occasionally.
    Bring to the boil and simmer until the milk has reduced by half.
2 Stir in the coconut, and continue stirring until the mixture forms a sticky lump in the middle of the pan.
3 Remove from the pan and spread on a greased toffee tray.
    Leave to cool and cut into cubes.

Makes 16 pieces.

Ramadan and Id-ul-Fitr

Regent's Park Mosque, London

Most religions have a period during which people put aside time to think about their beliefs and make their faith stronger. Very often people give up things or fast during these times. Just as Lent is the time for this in the Christian faith, so Ramadan is the time for Muslims to experience poverty and learn self-discipline.

Like the ancient Chinese calendar (see page 6), the Muslim calendar is based on the movements of the moon. This means that the Muslim year is ten days shorter than a Christian year. Eventually each Muslim month passes through all the seasons of the year. So Ramadan, although always the ninth month of the Muslim calendar, moves gradually through the different seasons of the year.

Ramadan is the most important time in the Muslim calendar. It lasts for a month and is dedicated to the month in which Muhammad had his first visions (see page 8).

Throughout the whole month of Ramadan Muslims do not eat or drink from dawn until sunset. If they get up early enough they may have an extremely early breakfast, and then nothing more until darkness sets in. They may not even drink any liquid during the hottest part of the day.

During Ramadan there are no parties or visiting and Muslims read the Quran and pray. They also try to avoid unkind or dishonest thoughts.

The end of Ramadan is celebrated with great enthusiasm. At the end of the month of Ramadan, the Muslim preacher, or Iman, announces to the worshippers in the mosque that Ramadan is over. He does this when he officially declares that the rim of the new moon has appeared over the horizon.

The festival is called the "Feast of the Breaking of the Fast", or Id-ul-Fitr, and for three days there is plenty to eat with special foods and lots of parties. Everyone visits friends and relations and they are expected to try some of the special foods being served. Cards and presents are exchanged. Everyone tries to have a complete set of new clothes for this event. Muslim children look forward to Id-ul-Fitr rather as Christian children look forward to Christmas.

However, Id-ul-Fitr is also a time for giving to the poor and every family sets aside a sum of money to give away.

Kheer

This is a sweet pudding often served at Id-ul-Fitr. It is made with concentrated milk. Sometimes it includes vermicelli, sometimes rice and vermicelli, and always plenty of flavourings, such as cardamoms, pistachio nuts, raisins, and cloves. In some areas suet is also included.

Here is a recipe from India.

Ingredients
15 g butter
50 g long grain rice
50 g very fine vermicelli
300 ml milk
50 g powdered milk
seeds from 3 cardamom pods, crushed
1 teaspoon rose water, if available
1 tablespoon flaked almonds or chopped pistachio nuts
50 g sugar
25 g raisins

Equipment
heavy-based saucepan
wooden spoon

Method

1 Melt the butter in a heavy-based pan and fry the rice and vermicelli until golden in colour.
2 Pour on the milk and bring to the boil. Simmer for 15 minutes.
3 Add the sugar, dried milk, raisins, and cardamoms.
   Return to the boil and continue to simmer for 15–20 minutes, stirring from time to time.
4 When the mixture thickens, add the rose water, if available, and spoon into a serving dish.
   Sprinkle nuts on top and serve warm or cold.

Serves 4–6.

Rosh Hashanah and Yom Kippur

Jews praying at the Wailing Wall in Jerusalem

There are no sour or bitter dishes at the table. This means that some people will not eat foods such as olives or aubergines. In the Middle East lemon juice is left out of the cooking, and Jews from Eastern Europe do not eat cucumbers, pickles, or horseradish at this meal.

Rosh Hashanah starts a solemn period of ten days during which Jews think about the way they have behaved during the past year and feel sorrow for any bad deeds. They examine their relationship with God and their fellow men, and ask for forgiveness.

At the end of this ten-day period is Yom Kippur. It is called the Day of Atonement. This is the day on which God's judgement for the next year is sealed. It is the holiest day in the Jewish year. The family eats before sundown, and then a twenty-four-hour fast begins. All Jews try to attend the synagogue at some time during the day to ask forgiveness for their sins.

At the special meal on the Eve of Yom Kippur, it is traditional for most Jews to eat chicken. Chicken and rice are eaten before fasts in many countries of the world. The foods are often cooked without pepper or salt. This helps to stop people getting indigestion or being quite so thirsty during the fast. The meal is always finished with a piece of bread and a drink of water. This is symbolic food for the fast.

Rosh Hashanah is the Jewish New Year. It usually falls in September or early October. 1987 is the year 5747 in the Jewish calendar. The people celebrate God's creation of the world and remember the Bible story of Abraham.

After prayers at the synagogue, Jewish families gather for a special meal. The table is covered with dishes using sweet foods such as raisins, carrots, and dates. Apples are eaten dipped in honey. They all represent hope for a "sweet" and happy year ahead.

After the fast is over the family come together for a meal. It may start off with something sweet such as another apple dipped in honey or a spoonful of home-made jam. This is followed by something salty such as herring, smoked salmon, or cured salmon with soured cream.

44

Carrot Kugel

Carrots are one of the few sweet-tasting vegetables and so they are very often used as a sweet vegetable dish served at Rosh Hashanah. In the USA, sweet potatoes are often used instead.

Strict Jews might leave the lemon juice out at Rosh Hashanah.

Ingredients
4 eggs, separated	225 g carrots
75 g sugar	juice of 1 orange
25 g butter	1 teaspoon lemon
1 small cooking apple	juice
grated rind of 1	50 g potato flour or
orange	cornflour

Equipment
grater	1-litre casserole or
basin	soufflé dish
egg whisk	

Method

1 Set the oven to 190°C/375°F/Gas 5, and grease a 1-litre casserole or soufflé dish.
2 Place the egg yolks in a bowl, and beat with the sugar until light and fluffy and pale in colour.
3 Very finely grate the carrot and apple, and squeeze out all the liquid.
4 Mix the grated carrot, apple, orange rind, orange and lemon juice, and flour.
   Mix well with the first mixture.
5 Whisk the egg whites until they are very stiff.
   Fold them into the carrot mixture.
6 Spoon into the greased casserole or soufflé dish.
7 Bake for 35 minutes or until golden brown.
   If you serve immediately the carrot kugel will be very puffed up.
   If you serve it cold it will fall a little.

Serves 4.

Chick-Peas with Carrots

This is a North African recipe. Chick-peas are a traditional food for Rosh Hashanah with Jews from this area.

Ingredients
1 large onion	225 g grated carrots
1 tablespoon cooking	or courgettes
oil	25 g sugar
400 g can chick-peas,	½ teaspoon
well drained	cinnamon
1 small potato	

Equipment
frying pan	grater
wooden spoon	1-litre casserole
kitchen knife	

Method

1 Set the oven to 200°C/400°F/Gas 6.
2 Peel and slice the onions, and fry in cooking oil until golden.
3 Mix the fried onions with the chick-peas and spoon into a casserole.
4 Peel and grate the carrots or courgettes and the potato.
   Place on top of the chick-peas.
   Sprinkle with sugar and cinnamon and cover with a lid.
5 Bake for 40 minutes until all the vegetables are tender.

Serves 4.

Harvest Festivals

Corn dollies

At one time, most people lived in the country and ate only what they could grow themselves. For them, the harvest time in August and September was the most important time of the year because their food for the winter months depended upon it.

In Medieval times, shortages of food were common. So the farmers did all they could to ensure a good crop. A loaf baked from the first corn of the season was brought to the church to be blessed.

At the end of the harvest the very last sheaf from the field was called the harvest queen or dolly. It was decorated with ribbon and taken to the farmhouse by the cheering farm workers. This harvest queen represented the spirit of corn. It was given the place of honour at the harvest supper. Afterwards the queen was kept safely until the next year when it would be burnt or ploughed back into the fields.

In later years the corn dollies were much smaller and were woven from the last few ears of corn gathered. These corn dollies were placed on the church altars at the harvest service. The figures were believed to bring new life to the seeds which provided the next year's crop.

In England the harvest home is still a popular festival. This usually takes place during September. Gifts of fruit and vegetables are placed round the altar for a special service of thanksgiving for a good crop. After the service the gifts are given to needy people in the parish.

The corn dollies of the past represented the corn or wheat harvest, but it is not only the cereal harvest which is celebrated. In some places, where the people rely on fishing to earn their living, there are "Blessings of the Waters" (or Boats) ceremonies. At North Shields, for example, the boats are blessed at an open air service on the quay. At other places the churches are decorated with fishing gear and nets.

There are similar harvest festivals in Europe. In Germany and Switzerland, September is the traditional month for the shepherds and cowherds to return to the valleys from the mountains. The animals are covered in flowers. The villagers put on their national costumes to welcome the procession of animals.

46

Stuffed Courgettes

The Jewish harvest festival is called Sukkot, or the Feast of the Tabernacles. It also remembers the journey of the Jews through the desert to the Promised Land. Huts are put up in the synagogues and in people's gardens, and the families gather in them to eat their meals.

This recipe comes from the Middle East and it uses both fruit and vegetables as well as meat. The latter may be left out and extra nuts added.

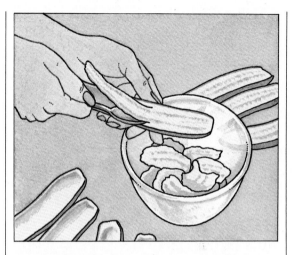

Ingredients

4 medium courgettes	1 small onion
50 g long grain rice	1 tablespoon freshly
1 tablespoon raisins	chopped parsley
4 dried apricots	1 teaspoon freshly
100 g minced lamb or	chopped mint
beef	salt and pepper
1 tablespoon pinenuts	150 ml tomato juice
or flaked almonds	

Equipment

kitchen knife	grater
baking tray or shallow	kitchen foil
casserole	teaspoon
basin	

Method

1 Set the oven to 190°C/375°F/Gas 5.
2 Wash the courgettes and cut in half lengthways.
   Scoop out a hollow along the length of each half using a teaspoon.
3 Retain the flesh from the centre of the courgette and chop very finely.
   Stir in the rice.
4 Finely chop the raisins, apricots, and nuts.
   Add to the mixture with the meat, herbs, and seasonings.
   Bind with a tablespoonful of the tomato juice. Mix well together.
5 Spoon some of the filling mixture over each half courgette, and press well down.
6 Place the stuffed courgettes in a baking tin or shallow casserole.
   Pour on the rest of the tomato juice.
   Cover with aluminium foil, and bake for 50 minutes until cooked through.

Serves 2.

Dussehra and Divali

Giant figures of the demon god ready for burning

Towards the end of October is the festival of Dussehra. This Hindu holiday celebrates the triumph of good over evil. The story told is that a legendary Indian prince, Rama, was helped by Sugriva, the monkey king, and by Hanuman, a monkey chief. Rama's wife, Sita, had been kidnapped by the evil demon king Ravana. After Hanuman had attacked Ravana's city, Rama managed to rescue her.

On the day of the festival, giant figures of the demon god are filled with fireworks and explosives. They are set up in large open spaces. They are then set alight by arrows of fire shot from the bow of a man dressed as the hero Rama.

The Indian town of Mysore is famous for its procession of elephants at this time. In Northern India, there are great floats on which the battles between Rama and Ravana are represented.

In England, Hindu families gather together. Married daughters often return to their parents' homes for feasting and singing and dancing. Brides and engaged couples look forward to this day because it is the custom for them to receive gifts from friends and relatives.

Divali comes shortly after Dussehra and may fall in October or November. It celebrates the victory of light over darkness. Many believe that Rama, on his return with Sita, was crowned on this day. The holiday is often called the "Festival of Lights" for homes are filled with lights. These used to be clay lamps but are now often candles or fairy lights.

These lights also welcome Lakshmi, the goddess of prosperity. She is said to visit the homes which are most brightly lit and to ensure their good fortune in the coming year. Rather like Father Christmas, she brings presents of sweetmeats which people give at this time.

Divali is also the commercial new year when businessmen open new accounts and prepare for the annual budget. They, too, may pray to Lakshmi for prosperity in the coming year. And for Sikhs the festival is important because one of the ten Gurus, Guru Hargobind, was set free at this time after being imprisoned by the Mogul Emperor.

Divali is a happy, carefree time when families and close friends get together. All the family's favourite foods are made and everyone enjoys themselves.

Vegetable Samosas

These tasty triangles may be served at the start of an Indian meal, or they may be served as snacks for visiting relatives or other guests. These snacks are traditionally deep fried. But they are just as good baked in the oven.

Ingredients

100 g plain flour
salt
1 teaspoon bicarbonate of soda or baking powder

3–3½ tablespoons water
1 tablespoon cooking oil
20 g butter

Filling:

1 onion
1 tablespoon cooking oil
450 g potatoes
1 carrot
100 g peas
2 teaspoons garam masala (see page 23)

1 teaspoon ground cumin
1 teaspoon ground coriander
3 tablespoons water
salt and pepper

Equipment

kitchen knife
saucepans
wooden spoon
tablespoon
teaspoon
rolling pin

baking tray
greaseproof paper
sieve
mixing bowl
pastry brush

Method

1 Start by making the filling.
    Peel and finely chop the onion, and fry in cooking oil until golden.
2 Peel and very finely dice the potatoes and carrots and add to the pan with the garam masala, coriander, cumin, water, and seasoning.
3 Stir the mixture and bring to the boil. Simmer for about 15–20 minutes, stirring from time to time, until the vegetables are tender and all the liquid has evaporated. Leave to cool a little.
4 Set the oven to 190°C/375°F/Gas 5 and grease the baking tray.
5 Next make the pastry.

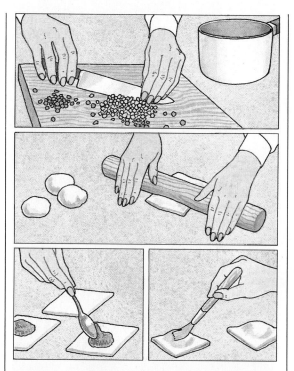

Start by sifting the flour, salt, and baking powder into a mixing bowl.
6 Melt the butter in a small pan, and pour over the flour.
    Add most of the water and mix to a dough, adding more water if necessary.
7 Place the dough on a floured surface, and knead for 2–3 minutes to make the dough more elastic.
8 Divide the mixture into 10 pieces and roll each one out into an 8 cm square.
9 Place a spoonful of the vegetable mixture on each square.
    Brush round the edges of the squares with a little water, and fold the pastry over to form triangles.
10 Brush each samosa with cooking oil, and place them on a greased baking tray.
11 Bake the samosas in the oven, until they are golden in colour. This will take about 20 minutes.
    Serve hot or cold.

Makes 10.

Hallowe'en

The evening before the festival of All Hallows, or All Saints, on 1st November is Hallowe'en. On All Saints' Day, the souls of the Christian faithful are honoured and remembered. The church chose this day because the people had always remembered the dead at this time of the year.

In pre-Christian times, many people believed in ghosts and witches, and they were often afraid of the dark. These beliefs continued until quite recently, and they are still remembered in some of the Hallowe'en customs. The traditions of wearing masks and of carving turnip faces lit with candles began as a way of frightening evil spirits away.

In ancient Celtic Britain, this time of the year was not only the beginning of winter, it was also the beginning of the New Year. Bonfires were lit on the hills to ward off the evil spirits and people gathered round the fires to feast and dance.

The ashes of the fires were sprinkled on the fields to ensure a good harvest in the coming year. This was intended as magic, but it probably did help the crops since the ashes contained chemicals which make the soil better.

Nowadays, we still light bonfires but these are usually only to burn the autumn leaves. In Britain, Guy Fawkes' Night has taken over the big bonfires. But in other countries there are still bonfires at Hallowe'en.

However, some of the old games are still enjoyed at Hallowe'en parties such as "Bobbing for apples" and "Swinging apples". In one game the apples float in water, and in the other they are hung on strings. The idea is to get a bite of one of the apples without touching it with anything but the teeth. Apple games go back to the Celtic belief that the branches of the apple tree helped dead souls to pass into their heaven.

Until the end of the last century Hallowe'en was sometimes known as "Mischief Night". Young people would play tricks on their neighbours. Today they will ask for a bribe to stop the tricks. They knock on the door, and ask "trick or treat?" Usually they are given a treat of sweets, home-made cakes or savouries.

Hallowe'en "Treats"

Here are a couple of savoury snacks which are good for serving at Hallowe'en parties or can be handed out as "treats".

Scotch Apples

Ingredients
1 apple
1 tablespoon flour
50 g sausage meat
2 eggs, beaten

175 g dried
  breadcrumbs
cooking oil

Equipment
kitchen knife
tablespoon
frying pan

Method

1. Quarter core and peel the apple.
   Cut into 12–14 small chunks.
2. Toss in flour and keep on one side.
3. Divide the sausage meat into 12–14 portions.
   Shape each portion round a piece of floured apple, making sure that the apple is completely covered.
   Shape into a ball.
4. Dip each ball in beaten egg and then coat with breadcrumbs.
5. Heat a little cooking oil in a frying pan and gently fry the balls for 8–10 minutes until golden brown and cooked through.
   Serve hot or cold.

Makes 12–14.

Nutty Bacon Roll-ups

Ingredients
80 g packet Cider
  Apple Stuffing Mix
25 g butter or
  margarine
125 ml boiling water

25 g chopped dry
  roasted peanuts
225 g rashers streaky
  bacon

Equipment
pudding basin
spoon

baking tray
kitchen knife

Method

1. Set the oven to 190°C/375°F/Gas 5.
2. Place the contents of the packet of stuffing mix in a basin.
   Pour on the boiling water and add the butter and nuts.
   Mix well together.
3. Cut off any rind from the bacon and stretch slightly by running the blunt edge of the knife along the bacon.
   Cut the rashers in half.
4. Divide the stuffing mixture into the same number of portions as there are bacon pieces.
5. Wrap each portion in a piece of bacon and place on a baking tray.
   Bake for 45 minutes.
   Serve hot or cold.

Makes about 16.

Guy Fawkes Night

Guido 'Guy' Fawkes and the rest of the gunpowder plotters

This festival is probably better known as 5th November or Bonfire Night, but it does owe its existence to a real Mr Guy Fawkes. He was a Catholic and also a soldier with a good knowledge of explosives.

Catholics were not very popular in the seventeenth century because they disagreed with the teachings of the Church of England and they wanted a Catholic king. They were not allowed to worship in their own way and they could not get the top jobs. Naturally they disliked this, and they wanted to change things.

In 1605, a group of Catholics with very strong feelings decided that they not only wanted to worship in their own way, they also wanted everyone else to join the Catholic church. They felt that the only way to achieve this would be to get rid of the King and Parliament.

Guy Fawkes joined the group of fanatics. They took a house next to the House of Lords and started to dig a tunnel. This took nearly a year to build, but they got through in the end. They brought in thirty-six barrels of gunpowder and stored it in a vault directly under the House of Lords.

The plan was for Guy Fawkes to set the fuse when the King and his son came to attend the opening of Parliament. However, one of the plotters wrote to his brother-in-law and warned him not to attend the opening. The letter was shown to the Government and the buildings were searched.

During the search, Guy Fawkes was found waiting to set fire to the gunpowder. He was taken to the Tower of London and tortured. Eventually, he and seven other plotters were found guilty of treason and executed.

Parliament decided that, since the plot had been discovered and no one had been hurt, November 5th should be a public holiday. It was to be a day of thanksgiving with bonfires and fireworks.

Since then, the cellars of the Houses of Parliament are carefully searched before the state opening of Parliament.

November 5th is no longer a public holiday, but children still make up figures to represent Guy Fawkes. And they still ask for a "penny for the Guy", though they probably expect a little more these days! The Guy is then burnt on the 5th of November bonfire.

52

Bonfire Potatoes and Chestnuts

Potatoes and chestnuts are the traditional foods to roast at this time.

Ingredients
4 large potatoes
450 g chestnuts

Equipment
potato skewers, if you
  have them
kitchen knife
grill pan

Method

1 Set the oven to 220°C/425°F/Gas 7.
2 Scrub the potatoes, and slit them along the top with a knife.
  Place on potato skewers, if using them.
3 Slit the domed surface of the chestnuts with a knife and place in a baking tray.
4 Place both the potatoes and the chestnuts in the oven.
5 Roast the chestnuts for 10–15 minutes and peel while they are still hot.
6 Roast the potatoes for 1 hour to 1¼ hours, depending on size.
7 For a slight charcoal taste, finish them both under a hot grill, turning frequently.
  When the skins begin to darken they are ready.
8 To fill the potatoes enlarge the slit in the top of the potato and make another cut at right angles to it.
  Open up a little by squeezing the potato with your hands inside the oven gloves.
  Fill with your favourite filling.

Suggested fillings for the potatoes

Quark low fat soft cheese or soured cream mixed with freshly chopped chives
Grated Cheddar cheese mixed with a little mustard or tomato ketchup
Yogurt mixed with tomato ketchup and finely chopped spring onions
Peanut butter mixed with yogurt and milk
Cottage cheese mixed with finely chopped crispy bacon
Hot frankfurter sausage and mustard with yogurt or soured cream

Thanksgiving

A rebuilt Mayflower at New Plymouth in America

This celebration falls on the fourth Thursday in November. Although it is an American holiday, it has its roots in Britain.

In 1620, a group of English and Dutch families sailed from Plymouth in the ship the *Mayflower*. They were leaving England because they wanted freedom from the Church of England. They wanted to worship on their own and in peace. They thought that they would find that peace and freedom in the New World of America. Their journey was a sort of pilgrimage and so these people are remembered as the "Pilgrim Fathers".

They landed in what is now Cape Cod Bay in Massachusetts and immediately started to build log cabins. They called this, their first town, Plymouth – after the port from which they had sailed.

As soon as spring came, they started to farm the land and sow their seeds. The native Indians were friendly and showed the Pilgrim Fathers how to grow the local crops of sweet potatoes, sweetcorn, and pumpkin. They also showed them how to catch and breed wild turkeys.

Because of this help from the Indians and their own hard work, the settlers were able to gather in their first harvest. Their leader invited the Indians to join them in a three-day festival of thanksgiving. The records of the time show that their celebrations began on a Thursday in November.

Since then Americans have celebrated Thanksgiving. It was officially proclaimed a public holiday in 1863. For some, the day includes a special church service in the morning. But everyone enjoys a Thanksgiving Dinner. All the traditional foods are included in the dinner. The centrepiece is the turkey, and there will be side dishes of sweet potatoes, sweetcorn, cranberry sauce, and a dessert of pumpkin pie.

Candied Sweet Potatoes

This is one of the traditional Thanksgiving dinner side dishes. Sweet potatoes are indeed sweet, and the addition of sugar makes them even sweeter. Serve with roast turkey or roast chicken.

Ingredients

600 g sweet potatoes
75 g Muscovado sugar
15 g butter
a little grated lemon rind
1 tablespoon lemon juice

Equipment

saucepan with lid
tablespoon
pudding basin
small casserole

Method

1 Set the oven to 190°C/375°F/Gas 5.
2 Peel and dice the sweet potatoes and place in a saucepan.
   Cover with water and bring to the boil. Simmer, covered for about 8–10 minutes until the potatoes are tender.
3 Drain well and spoon into a casserole.
4 Mix the sugar with the lemon rind and lemon juice, and spread this mixture over the top of the potatoes.
5 Dot the top with butter and bake for 35 minutes.

Serves 4.

Succotash

Indian corn or sweetcorn is the traditional basis for this dish. If you cannot find canned lima beans, use canned or frozen broad beans instead. Lima beans are green beans rather like broad beans.

Ingredients

25 g streaky bacon (optional)
1 dessertspoon plain flour
150 ml single cream
175 g canned or frozen sweetcorn
350 g canned or frozen lima beans or broad beans

Equipment

non-stick saucepan
dessert spoon
wooden spoon

Method

1 Dice the bacon and fry in the saucepan in its own fat until lightly browned.
2 Stir in the flour and the cream and bring to the boil, stirring all the time.
3 Add the well-drained sweetcorn and beans, and heat through gently, stirring from time to time with a wooden spoon. They will be ready after 5–8 minutes.

Serves 4.

Id-ul-Azha

Thousands of pilgrims praying near Mecca

Once in his or her lifetime, a Muslim must go on a pilgrimage to Mecca if at all possible. They should arrive there during the sacred month of Pilgrimage, or Dhu'l-Hijja, wearing a simple white garment. They should also fast during the day. In this way the differences between wealth and race are blotted out.

Once in Mecca the pilgrims must visit the Ka'bah. This is a cube-shaped building at the centre of the Grand Mosque, the most holy place for Muslims. In one corner is a holy Black Stone surrounded by silver. The Ka'bah has been a shrine since the time of Abraham. The pilgrims run seven times round the Ka'bah, each time kissing or touching the Black Stone. The crowds are now so great that most people have to be content with just looking at it.

Towards the end of the month of Pilgrimage the pilgrims must journey on foot for some distance away from Mecca, camping out each night at various holy places. At the end there is a sacrifice of many sheep or goats followed by a feast.

The rich provide the meat for those who cannot afford it.

The sacrifice may be in memory of Abraham who, in Muslim tradition, offered a sacrifice after building the Ka'bah in Mecca. The pilgrimage is ended by returning to Mecca.

In the past, many Muslims had very long and difficult journeys to get to Mecca. Today many pilgrims will go most of the way by air. The pilgrimage is still a duty but the poor and sick are not expected to carry out this duty.

However, the festival of Id-ul-Azha, or the Feast of Sacrifice, which marks the end of the month of Pilgrimage is very important to all Muslims, whether they have been on a pilgrimage or not. It lasts for four days, and starts with prayers at the mosque. Families club together to buy a sheep or cow, which is then killed according to Islamic law by the local halal butcher (see page 9). It is then cooked and divided between the families and the poor. It is a happy sociable time.

Lamb Kebabs

The easiest way to roast meat is over an open fire or under a grill. The meat will cook quite quickly and so it needs to be cut into small pieces to enable the heat to get to all parts of the meat. These pieces are threaded on to skewers to make kebabs.
This comes from a Middle Eastern recipe.

Ingredients
600 g lean lamb
125 g plain yogurt
1 teaspoon lemon
  juice

1 clove garlic
a little fresh root
  ginger (optional)
salt and pepper

Equipment
knife
bowl
skewers

Method

1 Cut the pieces of lamb into large cubes, and remove any fat or gristle.
2 Place in a bowl, and pour on the yogurt and lemon juice.
3 Chop the garlic very finely and grate the peeled root ginger if using.
  Add to the bowl, and toss the meat in the yogurt mixture.
4 Leave to stand for 20 minutes or longer, if there is time available.
5 Thread the meat onto four skewers.
6 Place under a hot grill, and cook for 10 minutes, turning the skewers three or four times during cooking.
7 Sprinkle with a little salt and pepper just before serving.
  Serve with boiled rice (see page 9) or pitta bread, and salad.

Serves 4.

St. Nicholas' Day

St. Nicholas

The great present-giving festival in most countries of Northern Europe is not Christmas Day but St. Nicholas' Day on 6th December. All the celebrations centre on children, for St. Nicholas is seen as the patron saint of children.

St. Nicholas was a much-loved bishop who lived in Myra in Asia Minor in the fourth century AD. He loved both poor people and children. He was a generous man who tried to keep his good deeds quiet. He died on 6th December.

In Holland he is known as Sinterklaas. But despite the fact that his name sounds similar to Santa Claus, he is quite different. Instead of a bright red cloak, St. Nicholas is dressed in the stately robes of a bishop. He is believed to travel by boat, not by reindeer sleigh, and he is accompanied by his faithful servant, Peter.

Once he arrives in the country of his destination, St. Nicholas rides a white horse over the rooftops and visits all the children's homes. Peter carries a huge sack of toys for those children who were well behaved during the previous year.

Preparations start a week or more ahead. Before going to bed children put out bread, hay, and a carrot for St. Nicholas' horse. Next morning the food has gone, and there may be a little present or a bag of sweets.

On the big evening itself the whole family gather and in Holland they sing St. Nicholas songs in anticipation of his visit. Then a knock on the door is heard, and the saint enters in full bishop's robes with a staff and a long white beard. Of course, he is an uncle or friend of the family dressed up for the occasion.

After being welcomed by the head of the family he asks Peter for his "Golden Book" in which everybody's good and bad deeds are recorded. As he gives out the presents he praises or tells off the adults and children alike.

Dutch St. Nicholas Biscuits

These biscuits are called speculaas, and you can see them on sale in every shop in Holland at this time of the year. However, they are quite easy to make. Make them in large rounds or if you have time, cut them into oval shapes and mark in St. Nicholas' beard and flowing robes.

Ingredients
100 g plain flour
1 teaspoon baking powder
¼ teaspoon salt
¼ teaspoon ground cinnamon
pinch ground nutmeg
pinch ground cloves
50 g brown sugar
50 g butter or margarine
1 tablespoon milk
8 blanched almonds

Equipment
kitchen knife
mixing bowl
baking sheet

Method

1 Place all the dry ingredients in a bowl and add the butter cut into small pieces.
2 Add the milk and knead to a smooth dough.
3 Roll out on a floured surface and shape into a round or cut into St. Nicholas shapes.
4 Place the large round or the individual biscuits on a greased baking sheet. Cut the round into eight wedges.
5 Press an almond into the top of each biscuit or wedge.
6 Bake at 220°C/425°F/Gas 7 for 7 minutes.
7 Reduce the heat to 170°C/325°F/Gas 3, and cook for a further 25 minutes.

Makes up to 16.

Hanukkah is the Jewish Festival of Lights. It lasts for eight days and is held some time in early December. The exact date changes from year to year because the start of the Jewish calendar also changes each year.

Hanukkah is a time of great happiness and joy. It is held to remember a miracle which took place in Israel over 2,000 years ago. At that time Israel, or Judea as it was called then, was ruled by the Syrian king, Antiochus.

He was not a Jew and he would not allow the Jews to worship their own god in the holy Temple in Jerusalem. Instead he sacrificed pigs to the Greek gods to make the Temple unholy for the Jews. He also tried to make them worship Zeus and other Greek gods.

This made the Jews very angry indeed and instead of giving in they decided to fight the Syrian king. They were led by a man named Judah and his brothers. They were greatly outnumbered by their enemies and they hardly had any weapons. But they still managed to defeat the king and his soldiers.

Their first action on gaining victory was to clean and re-dedicate the Temple. To do this they needed to re-light the Temple Menorah, or light, which was meant to burn all the time. This light represented the eternal light of the spirit. However, they could only find enough oil for one day but they decided to go ahead and light the Menorah anyway. Their faith was rewarded, for the oil lasted for eight days until new oil could be prepared.

Hanukkah is the Hebrew word for dedication. Every year Jewish families light their own Menorah at home in memory of that time in Jerusalem. The Menorah holds eight candles. On the first evening of Hanukkah only one candle is lit. On the second night two candles are lit and so on until, on the eighth night, all the candles are burning brightly.

The candle lighting ceremony takes place in the evening, usually before the evening meal. This meal always includes fried foods, and this often means Pancakes or Potato Latkes. The oil used to fry these traditional pancakes is, of course, a reference to the cleaning and re-dedication of the Temple.

Potato Latkes

There are probably as many different recipes for this dish as there are Jewish families making them for Hanukkah. Serve with apple sauce.

Ingredients
2 large potatoes
1 very small onion
1 small egg
cooking oil

1 tablespoon plain
    flour or
    breadcrumbs
salt and pepper

Equipment
grater
bowl
fork

frying pan
fish slice

Method

1 Peel the potatoes and place in a bowl of water to stop them going black.
2 Grate the onion on the large holes of the grater into a bowl.
3 Grate one potato on the large holes of the grater and one on the smaller holes.
  Mix all the potato with the onion.
4 Press out as much liquid as you possibly can.
5 Mix in the egg, flour, and salt, and pepper.
6 Heat about 3–4 tablespoons of cooking oil in a frying pan and drop in one tablespoonful of the potato mixture.
  Cook on one side for 3–4 minutes until golden in colour.
  Turn over with a fish slice and cook the other side for the same period of time.
7 Keep the Latkes hot while you use up the rest of the mixture.

Serves 2–3.

Variation

Replace one potato with grated carrot or grated courgettes.
If you are using courgettes add another two teaspoons of flour or breadcrumbs.
Continue as for the basic recipe.

Apple Sauce

Ingredients
1 lb cooking apples
1 teaspoon lemon
  juice

1 tablespoon water or
  apple juice

Equipment
knife
saucepan with lid

Method

1 Peel, core, and quarter the apples.
  Cut each quarter into slices.
2 Place in the saucepan with all the other ingredients, and cover with a lid.
  Place on a medium heat and bring to the boil.
  Reduce the heat and simmer for 10–15 minutes until the apples have "fallen".

Serves 2–3.

Christmas

Christmas is the Christian celebration of the birth of Jesus Christ. The story of Christmas tells how Jesus was born in a stable at Bethlehem. The baby and his parents were visited there by the three wise men, or kings. This story is often illustrated by home-made cribs showing the nativity scene. These are displayed in church, at school, or at home.

We do not know the actual day on which Jesus was born. But 25th December is the day chosen to celebrate His birth. The new festival took the place of earlier pagan festivals. Many of the early customs still survive.

Pagan people believed that holly was lucky and that mistletoe was sacred and could cure all kinds of ills. For some Christians the holly has come to represent the crown of thorns that Jesus wore when he was crucified.

The custom of giving presents also goes back much further than St. Nicholas or the wise men's presents to the Christ child. This was the time of the year when the Romans gave each other presents.

For Christians, the most important part of the Christmas festival is the church service. At midnight on Christmas Eve, the church bells ring out all over the Christian world. Inside, candles light up the crib and carols are sung.

Christmas Day itself is a time for the family to get together for a special meal. The main course of the traditional Christmas feast is now a turkey. But this is a fairly new tradition. Up until the last century its place would have been taken by a boar's head or a large joint of beef.

Plum porridge was the forerunner of today's Christmas pudding. It was very much more runny than today's pudding. The spices, hidden coins, and flaming brandy of the modern pudding remind us of the myrrh, gold, and frankincense given to Jesus by the Wise Men.

Mincemeat and Mince Pies

Mince pies used to be very different. They were actually mutton pies seasoned with spices brought back from the Holy Land by the crusaders.

They were oval-shaped to resemble the manger and a small piece of pastry was laid across the top to represent the child Jesus. Today the only remaining meat in the pie is the suet in the mincemeat.

Mincemeat is better if it is made in advance and kept for a few days. If the mincemeat is to be kept longer still, it needs sherry in place of the water. It will keep for up to a month.

Mincemeat

Ingredients

50 g cooking apples	50 g shredded suet
50 g currants	25 g chopped nuts
50 g raisins	100 g demerara sugar
50 g sultanas	½ teaspoon mixed
25 g glacé cherries	spice
25 g chopped mixed peel	1 tablespoon water or sherry

Equipment
kitchen knife
bowl
jam jar

Method

1 Peel, core, and finely chop the apples.
2 Wash and finely chop the dried fruit.
3 Mix in a large bowl and blend in the rest of the ingredients.
   Leave to stand for 24 hours.
4 Pack in a 700 g jam jar.
   Cover with a screw-top lid.

Makes about 600–700 g.

Mince Pies

Ingredients

400 g frozen shortcrust pastry, thawed	600–700 g mincemeat (see left)
milk	juice of 1 lemon

Equipment

rolling pin	teaspoon
lemon squeezer	bun tray

Method

1 Set the oven to 200°C/400°F/Gas 6.
2 Roll out just over half the pastry, and use to line about 12–14 bun tins.
   Cut the pastry with pastry cutters or with a glass of the right size.
3 Fill with spoonfuls of mincemeat.
   Add a little lemon juice to each one.
4 Roll out the rest of the pastry, and cut 12–14 lids to fit the pies.
5 Brush the edges of the pastry with a little water, and put the lids in place.
6 Brush the tops with a little milk, and bake for 20–25 minutes until golden in colour.

Makes 10–12.

Index of Recipes

Acknowledgements

The publishers would like to thank the following for permission to reproduce photographs:

Barnaby's Picture Library p.14; BBC Hulton Picture Library p.36; Bridgeman Art Library p.38 (top); Trustees of the British Museum p.40; Camerapix Hutchison p.8; Roger Charlesson p.24, p.46; Douglas Dickins p.1; E.T. Archive Ltd. p.38 (bottom); Mary Evans Picture Library p.26, p.52; Format Photographers/Maggie Murray p.50; Hong Kong Government Office p.34; Impact Photographers/ Alain le Garsmeur p.6; Rob Judges p.53; NAAS/Abdal Ghaffur Mould p.56; Netherlands Board of Tourism, p.58; Ann & Bury Peerless p.18 (top and bottom), p.22, p.48; Brian & Sally Shuel p.4, p.62; Spectrum Colour Library p.10 (top), p.28 (bottom), p.42, p.44, p.54; Stop Press © Jane Appleby-Dean p.10 (bottom); Homer Sykes p.30; ZEFA Picture Library p.12, p.16, p.28 (top), p.32, p.60.

Spices were supplied by Lion Foods Ltd.

Recipe photographs are by Steven Lee (except p.24/5 and p.53).

Illustrations are by Patricia Capon.

Cover illustration is by Nancy Anderson.